Around the World

I0879078

Homes Around the World

By Meg Gaertner

level 2

little blue readers

www.littlebluehousebooks.com

Copyright © 2021 by Little Blue House, Mendota Heights, MN 55120. All rights reserved. No part of this book may be reproduced or utilized in any form or by any means without written permission from the publisher.

Little Blue House is distributed by North Star Editions:
sales@northstareditions.com | 888-417-0195

Produced for Little Blue House by Red Line Editorial.

Photographs ©: Shutterstock Images, cover, 4, 6–7, 8–9, 13, 15, 17, 18, 20–21, 23, 24 (bottom left); iStockphoto, 10, 24 (top left), 24 (top right), 24 (bottom right)

Library of Congress Control Number: 2020900829

ISBN
978-1-64619-185-7 (hardcover)
978-1-64619-219-9 (paperback)
978-1-64619-287-8 (ebook pdf)
978-1-64619-253-3 (hosted ebook)

Printed in the United States of America
Mankato, MN
082020

About the Author

Meg Gaertner enjoys reading, writing, dancing, and being outside. She lives in an apartment in Minnesota.

Table of Contents

Many Kinds **5**

Different Shapes **11**

Coming Home **19**

Glossary **24**

Index **24**

Many Kinds

People live in different kinds of homes.

This home has stilts.
They hold the home
above the ground.

stilt

These homes
are underground.
They keep people cool.

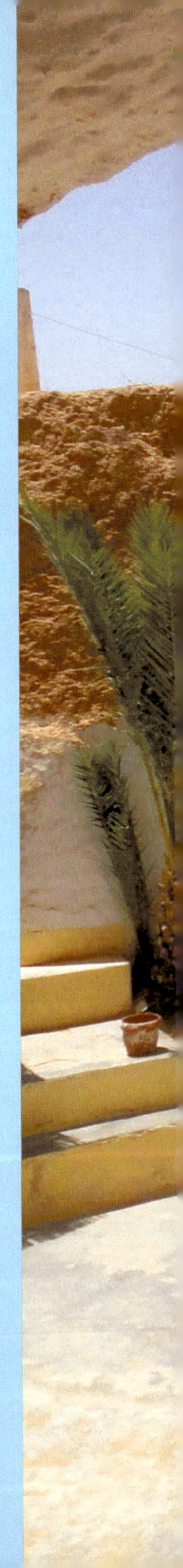

Different Shapes

This home has a cone shape.

These homes are tall
and narrow.
They are close together.

This home is round.
Dry leaves cover the top
of the home.

This home is round.

It is a kind of tent.

tent

wheel

Coming Home

This home is very small.

It has wheels.

This home is a boat.

It moves around on

the river.

boat
river

Homes can look very different. But people around the world enjoy coming home.

Glossary

river

tent

stilts

wheels

Index

B

boat, 20

S

stilts, 6

T

tent, 16

W

wheels, 19